More praise for *War / Torn*

"Written in emotional and visceral language,
Hasan Namir's poems are bold, exploring the harsh
expectations of masculinity, the battles we wage in
our worlds large and small, and the holiness in desire.
In these poems there are no dichotomies, but the full
breadth of human experience, from the roughest to
the most tender of moments."
—Dina Del Bucchia, author of *It's a Big Deal!*

"*War / Torn* collides and bridges worlds of chaos
and love and sex and violence and lust and hope.
Beautiful, heartbreaking, and an unflinching look at
the terrifying reality of homophobia, war, and shame.
A collection of poems that asks how we reconcile
all the parts of our identities and histories, with the
sincerity and caring touch only Hasan can bring to it."
—Daniel Zomparelli, founder of *Poetry Is Dead*

"Precise and relentless in its interrogation of doctrine,
intimacy, and masculinities, Hasan Namir's poetry is
informed by violence and infused with tenderness.
War / Torn slashes perception to ribbons and cradles
the remains."
—Carleigh Baker, author of *Bad Endings*

War / Torn

War / Torn

Hasan Namir

BOOK*HUG PRESS 2019

FIRST EDITION

The production of this book was made possible through the generous assistance
of the Canada Council for the Arts and the Ontario Arts Council. Book*hug Press
also acknowledges the support of the Government of Canada through the Canada
Book Fund and the Government of Ontario through the Ontario Book Publishing
Tax Credit and the Ontario Book Fund.

 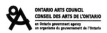

Book*hug Press acknowledges the land on which it operates. For thousands of years
it has been the traditional land of the Huron-Wendat, the Seneca, and most recently,
the Mississaugas of the Credit River. Today, this meeting place is still the home to
many Indigenous people from across Turtle Island, and we are grateful to have the
opportunity to work on this land.

LIBRARY AND ARCHIVES CANADA CATALOGUING IN PUBLICATION

Title: War / torn / Hasan Namir.
Other titles: War slash torn
Names: Namir, Hasan, 1987– author.
Description: First edition. | Poems.
Identifiers: Canadiana (print) 20190075325 | Canadiana (ebook) 20190075333

ISBN 9781771664936 (softcover)
ISBN 9781771664943 (HTML)
ISBN 9781771664950 (PDF)
ISBN 9781771664967 (Kindle)

Classification: LCC PS8627.A536 W37 2019 | DDC C811/.6—dc23

PRINTED IN CANADA

CONTENTS

AGAINST THE WALL

THE MORNINGS I KISSED SADDAM

JANNAH

LOTEE & SHATH

THE STORY OF A MAN

This is 1990

    This is the Gulf War

        This is the story of a man
        who dresses like a man

        who talks like a man
        who eats like a man

This is 2011

    This is another war

        This is the story of a man
        who dresses like a man

        who talks like a man
        who eats like a man

This is 1990

    This is when I held on to you
        in the story of a man

        who walks like a man
        who pees like a man

This is 2011

      This is when I hoped you would
                    in the story of a man

                who farts like a man
                who drives like a man
                who shits like a man

This is 1990

      This is when I struggled for you
                    in the story of a man

                who pays like a man
                who drinks like a man
                who comes like a man

This is 2011

      ]This is when you fought with them
                    in this story of a man

                who drives like a man
                who cries like a man

THE WORST

My legs were hanging in the air.

Words were like the chafe of a rope
against the throat. I hadn't understood
what it meant to be different, to stand
out as the worst of humanity, worse
than the gutter, worse than the worst
sin. Like a dagger in its scabbard, pushing
at the skin, I saw half my soul, waiting

on the other side. I had committed
the worst sin, worse than marrying
a Christian. I was a Shath, a fucking
queer. And a Lotee, a damned faggot.
I want to have a family. How hard
can that be?

A man and a man and a baby.

PAIRS

Two pairs of legs
Over the bed
Lotee & Shath
Faggot & Queer
Fuck each other
Sodomites in saffron
Too many gazes
Masjid yawning in almond
Two cock-sucking angels
The Caspian Sea glistens
By a broken window
A mother watches
Two boys come on each other
A breeze sifts their eyes open
A God can't watch
Allah can't watch

THE PIANO

Hold my piano hands and blow
          Slurp my semen and my children
          Push deeper and make me soar

Fuck me kindly and make me torn
          Taste this milky blood and inhale
          Make me a man. Make me home

Bend me in half and blow
          Let me, Lotee, jump and send my Salam
          Make me snort and fly high

LOTEE & SHATH

I.

Do you remember?
Summer
2003
Mesopotamia

2.

Today is holy Friday
We must all be pure and clean
We must wash our sins and grime
Because in Iran we don't have
Homosexuals like your homosexuals

3.

The rays of the sun
Fighting the young soldiers
Lotee & Shath

4.

The hellish hairs of fire
Leave no rash on me

5.

You're a man
What's a man?

6.

Halal is just a word
Back chest arm

7.

Because today is holy
We must wash our crimes
You are a man
Am I a man's man?

8.

The desert horses neigh
Friends jump into the unknown
Land on the Fire of Allah
The scent of saffron

9.

If you remember
their eyes
fear and jealousy

10.

Allahu Akbar
Bang Bang Bang

11.

I'm the Lotee
Lonely hand
Bloodied heart
Grip the flag

12.

Then I remember to remember

Lotee & Shath
Envy their namesakes
Needles and pink

JUST ANOTHER LOTEE

Karar Nushi's hair was blond
Long straight green eyes
Glowing on social media
Shot in the head twice

Muhammad Al Mutairi was Shia
Not that it mattered
He was just another Lotee
Stabbed to death

The other man was anonymous
Shot within two days
People of Lut be damned
Kill all the Lotees & Shaths

It could have been me
I am just another Lotee

I could have been stabbed to death
I could have been shot within two days
I could have been shot in the head

I want to see my mother

KHUSRAH

[Through a fractured window
I am overwhelmed by the revolt.
Close the window.]

[This is my mother war-stricken and restless,
carrying a photo album in her hand.]

[A book of coloured spaces,
I look through these photos,
forced to choose. I let out a sigh
over the flag gagging the pole.]

[Mama, you knew.
Help me, son, I want to see your kids.
She poses like a wax mannequin,
stunned near the radiator.]

[Through her eyes I am consumed
by years of family history.
I am about to claw the roots
of the olive tree.
I am now a Khusrah.]

CHILDREN OF ADAM

O child of Adam the one who was executed in Iran
You are the descendant of the Prophet in blood
O child of mercy the one who was pushed off the tower
You happened to be Christian Iraqi, Allah yerhamak
O child of El-Sayed who was stabbed to death
May Allah forgive your souls
You paid the price for being Lotee

BLOOD SPOT

EID

It's Eid day today / a kiss here a kiss there
Eid day to celebrate a bloody feast

Mama says her prayers / Baba says his prayers
Brother has a knife ache / bleeding fingers
She holds my head / Bebe / says her prayers

                                                                                  Allahu Akbar

It's Eid day today / a kiss here a kiss there

Mama says her prayers / Baba says his prayers
Brother has a knife ache / bleeding fingers
She kisses my head / Bebe / says her prayers

                                                                                  Allahu Akbar

Eid day to celebrate but a bloody feast

Mama says her prayers / Baba says his prayers
Brother had a knife ache / bleeding fingers
She cuts my head / Bebe / ends her prayers

                                                                                  Allahu Akbar

It's Eid day today / a kiss here a kiss there

BLOOD SPOT

An exterior shot of rain / pearls of water against asphalt / a mother / fragile
walks / in red patterned cloth / photographs of strangers in hand / pick one
and let me see the sun / don't be stubborn my torn one / a son / eyes open /
the photographs were blank / if I didn't choose any of them / am I still your
used martyr? / Yes you are my flesh / my blood spot, I slay for you / Mama,
you need this / truth I must say I am Lotee/ a mother breaks / a son wipes her
tears / I wash my hands with sun / Am I never going to see her thirst again? /
I am Shath, Mama / interior shot / shrapnel in the chest / bits of sun / bits of
saffron

THE BALL

The soccer ball / against my face
I was not / into sports / Basketball dribbles
Popularity smiles / This is how they treat difference
They laughed / them at me / I cried / the Lotee / me
They picked their teams / I was always chosen / last

1990 (I)

Every day and night I dreamt of Father
I remember 1990, I was three, Father loved me
I remember 1998, we left our country for Canada

Regrets
Execution
Dirt
Kill
Allah
Lotee
Shath
Muhammed
Ali
Iraqi
Canadian

1987

1987. What do you remember?
Our family lost 13
Oh and you
You were born

THE STORY OF A CHILD

This is the story of a child,
pearls of rain over azan,
echoes from a call to prayer.

This is the story of a child,
the kidney of Adam, the umbilical
cord that holds twin breaths.

Sperm is injected and
two become one.

This is the story of a child.

Mother's cervix open,
in combustible dust,
in carbon monoxide,
in waves of labour.

This is the story of a child and
Eve, a surrogate mother.

(O my Lord! How shall I have a son
when no man hath touched me?)

This is the story of a child born
a hyphenated angel,
Muslim-Sikh,
Inshallah-Waheguru.

DRIP...DRIP...DRIP...

A single drip from one umbilical cord Three fleshed bodies from one Three separate reasons Two sisters and one faggot Sometimes I hear them make fun of me Don't call me a fag! Sorry, it won't happen again I look down and I see them disapprove of me Fag is worse than dirt, Baba says I looked down at the dead, prayed for them I looked down and I saw shame Faces look down at you, shaming you, shaming your family What do you now then? When I need you, I look down and then I see faces looking at me, looking against me, looking at me like that's a thing I can't bear it anymore I just want to be buried or suffocated

1990 (II)

Two words
Arms open
Too late

1990 (III)

My grandfather—the general
My father—the engineer
My uncle—the doctor
My aunt—the teacher
My mother—the engineer
Myself—the Lotee

THE FAMILY OF THE PROPHET

O Allah bless Muhammad
and His family
Muhammad and Ali
My brother O brother
Like their namesake
Allahu Akbar
Lotee & Shath
My brother O brother
We drip and burn
My tears O brother
Many blessings to you
Muhammad when I pray
They drip and burn
Shath & Lotee

WHEN I TOLD YOU

Mama the air sparkles with gay flitters that blind our deceptive eyes / metallic old blood of a butchered animal / Tiny butterflies mourning the death of a Lotee / He whom you assumed I was that I am not Baba / I pant when I think of the water asthmatic particles hang down my throat / under the bridge that separates us and why / You only look over in fear of those who watch

Mama it was Baghdad when I put my cousin's cock in my mouth
He played with my nipples / I was horny
He was 24 / I was 10
You walked right in and saw
You spoke as if you saw nothing
Baba when I told you

WHERE IS MY SON?

Dead sperm
The olive tree
The Tigris river
Abu Ghraib prison
Gulf War
Where is he?
The little soul who floats in the heavens
Pure-bred and white-covered
From the hanging gardens of Babylon
To the respected Abbasid empire of Baghdad
Breathtaking and skin-numbing
To the Abbasid empire of Baghdad
It snowed on 9/9/1987 and you came
A drizzle of white snow where is he?
Where is my son who hides in a dress?

WHERE IS THE SNOW?

The son of Lotee
Where is the snow?
Over there
Over here in front of me when I look
I walk outside and I see a faggot
Where is my son?
Where is my son, my dear sisters?
I can't find him
I keep looking and looking
O God, where is my son?
Look for the olive tree
Mother, where is my son?
I drizzle a drop of snow
It floats from the seawall
Over the Pacific Ocean
It flies and looks for my son
The metaphor of His Light
Is that of *a niche in which*
The lamp inside a glass
The glass like a brilliant star
Lit from a blessed tree
An olive neither of the east
Nor the west
Its oil giving off light
Even if no fire touches the light
Light Upon Light
Allah guides

DIRT

[Dirt is the disorder Baba believes / my life has been dirt / he sends me to a dirt doctor in order to create order / The doctor digs and jigsaw / pieces fall through his eyes into my skin / they burn the thick part of flesh / Where do you see yourself? / Not a reflection but in the dirt / I smile back / my voice echoes through the caverns in my father's hands / in his pockets / my hand over my mouth]

EVERYTHING'S THE SAME

Nothing but He
He is still home
He is the same as the day before
Nothing has changed
Baba's arms are flailing
Tomorrow is another day
After yesterday's talk
He wears less shiny clothes
His hands are quiet now
He holds himself
Hands in his pockets
He must be a man's man
Before he leaves for war
His father gives him a look
A look that is a fist
Today is not the day
When will it be?
A hand over his mouth
Did you want to say something?
I love you, Baba
Hands in his pockets
He leaves the house
Today is still today

BLOOD BROTHER

Slaughter The cries of a young Lotee This is the Blood that seeps from a torn piece of flesh In 1996 He was eight Don't tell anyone about this sad pathetic little boy or else I will hurt you He pushed deeper and deeper It became a painless numb Yet a flesh forever torn His lips vomited sweat An animal slaughtered on Eid day Whatever happened to honouring Blood No What are you afraid of? His Blood sprayed from the umbilical cord He cried in the arms of His brother He stripped His clothes and pushed Quite the birthday gift He came out of His mother's womb and cried He was pink and red Tomorrow He will be nine My brother My brother He sliced the umbilical cord and threw Me back in the Blood

AGAINST THE WALL

NOTHING GREATER (I)

The family fails

Run!

I let you run
What about you?

I will see you over there
What about you?

In God's Jannah
There is nothing greater than Allah

I have no regrets no fear
I feel no pain pain I feel
Shath Lotee Lotee Shath

No I feel no pain but fear
I feel no fear but fear I feel

Push me already Push Push
Push Push Push Push Push

Let me Lotee let me Shath

Push—
Let me sink and rise—

Allahu Akbar
Allahu Akbar

MOSQUE/INTERNAL

MOSQUE
EVENING
INTERNAL

Fadi stares at himself in the mirror

SHEIKH: Homosexuality is unlawful in Islam / It is neither accepted by
the state nor by the Islamic Society / Quran clearly states that it is unjust
unnatural transgression ignorant criminal and corrupt / I have collected
verses from the Quran which clearly show us this haram... (Fade out)

FLASHBACK
ADAM'S BEDROOM
INTERNAL

*Fadi and Adam kiss passionately on the bed,
tongues interlocked*

SHEIKH: If two men among you commit indecency / punish them both / If
they repent and mend their ways, let them be/ God is forgiving and merciful

MOSQUE
EVENING
INTERNAL

Yusef scans the area and looks for Fadi

SHEIKH: God says / You lust after men instead of women / Truly you are a
degenerate people

MOSQUE
WASHROOM
EVENING
INTERNAL

Fadi washes his hands and face and glimpses his own reflection

ADAM'S BEDROOM
EVENING

Fadi and Adam continue to kiss shirtless / soaked / in sweat / breathless

SHEIKH: Do you commit indecency with your eyes open lustfully seeking
men instead of women? Surely you are ignorant people

INSIDE
THE
CAR

Yusef gazes at them through his window
Fadi is down on Adam, who moans, eyes wide shut
Yusef's face a masquerade filled with shock and anger
Yusef's car drives past them
Fadi stops and looks up at Adam

ADAM: Shit I hope someone wasn't watching or anything

HIGH SCHOOL THEATRE
NIGHT
INTERNAL

Among the crowded audience, Yusef sits all alone, uncomfortable and nervous
Fadi and Adam wear dress shirts and dress pants, stand together
Behind them is a background that illustrates a street in Verona

ADAM: Hand me a torch / I hate dawdling along / Because I have a heavy heart I will carry the light

FADI: No, Romeo / We want you to dance too

ADAM: Not me / I assure you / You have on dancing shoes with light soles

Fadi draws his sword against Stuart, a high school student, a drama diva
In the audience, Yusef puts his hand on his jeans pocket. His hand shakes in fear

FADI: Tybalt / you rat catcher / will you come with me?

In the audience, Yusef's hand shakes as it reaches for the gun

ADAM: Mercutio / put up your sword

On the stage, Fadi and Stuart clash

ADAM: Draw your sword / Benvolio Ward off their weapons Gentlemen this is shameful! / Stop this outrageous behaviour!

Stuart stabs Fadi with one thrust as a GUNSHOT fills the air
Fadi falls in Adam's arms, blood splashes everywhere
Yusef cries drops the gun / His hand continues to shake / He tries to catch his breath

ADAM: Fadi!

There are screams and cries within the audience
Fadi's body rests in Adam's hands lifeless. Adam cries over his body
Lotee/Shath

NOTHING GREATER (II)

Dirty socks and stale air
The moan of a lover's piano
A sperm-shone rusty surface
The caress of his haram skin

Inna lillahi wa inna ilayhi raji'un
And there is nothing greater than Allah

A double standard
A greater heart than theirs

Run, habibi, run
Don't stop
Keep running
Don't let them
Please don't
Don't let them
Run, habibi, run

Inna lillahi wa inna ilayhi raji'un
There is nothing greater than Allah

And another word
Yet another
It all means the same

Man to Man
Shath Lotee
Lotee Shath

LOTEE

You created the world in seven days

You created angels, demons, and you created me

You created birds, animals, and them

You created stars, the sun, and us

You created earth and the sky, and them

And I will kneel down and pray
I will give to the poor and help
I will kiss the earth and cry
When am I allowed to be

And I remember Lot
When he said to his people
Verily, ye approach men
No one in the world anticipated

HOW TO KILL HOMOSEXUALS

1. Rub surfaces with lube
2. Condemn them *Shayateen Lut*
3. Shame them
4. Strike them with shoes
5. Let your spit drip
6. Ease the tension
7. Whip their flesh
8. Stone them to death
9. Gently push a finger or two
10. Hang them until
11. Push in
12. Turn them out

YOU'RE GONE

Sit on a bench / Face the hybrid river / Ducks swim in Salam This is our
favourite spot / Arabian accent thick / The Lotees together / One accepts and
understands / It has been four years since I left you / Today the words sound
terroristic / Drums beat / Ears crush / Scream some stupid rock & roll song
/ Why did you bring me here? / The classical concerto A violinist's orgasmic
orchestra / I need another chance / You need to move on / Will you play at
my wedding? / The violin strings wail / I'll play / You pinched in my chin The
screeching unnerving cellos

THE BLASPHEMOUS

He stood against the wall / a Quran in hand / The rain beats and burns / He searched for Allah / He wanted answers / You're not my son and I don't want to see you anymore / Get out of my house / He just wants to live / He said to his people / How could you commit such an abomination publicly / How can you witness such disgrace? / You practise sex with men lustfully instead of women / Evict the Lotees and preserve the pure / He tore the Quran in little pieces / He threw the pieces in the air / There were eyes to see pieces of human flesh / There were eyes to see the Lotees flying in the air and the sun and the moon and the stars / Allahu Akbar

THE FIVE PILLARS

1. Shahadah

There is no God but Allah
and Muhammad is His messenger
I profess my belief in you
I fuck Lotee
Shath fucks me

2. Salat

Salat al-fajr: dawn,
before sunrise
Salat al-duhr:
midday, after the sun passes its highest
Salat al-asr:
the late part of the afternoon
I perform my prayer
Salat al-maghreb:
just after sunset
My thoughts are with him
Salat al-isha:
between sunset and midnight
I'm in love with the Lotee

3. Zakat

I have given charity
I worshipped
I obeyed
I love Shath

4. Sawm

Ramadan
My throat dry
I fast and break it
My semen was white

5. Hajj

I could go to Saudi Arabia
My images all over the Net
I have been labelled
Shath & Lotee
In my karaoke of faith

PIANO (II)

My hands ache when I play the piano
Piano hands that will marry the dust
Dust that seeps through the keys
Keys the whites of my eyes
My eyes pinprick in the pain
The pain of Lotee burning
Lotee burning into ash reborn
Fingers caress habibi and my soulmate
My heart and my habibi caress fingers
This is just a phase a stage of life

BLASPHEMY

You approach the males of the world
and forsake those whom the Lord created
for you and your mates blasphemed
with men's filth
struggled to catch breath
I'm married
Most surely you are guilty of an indecency
Do you come unto the males?
Heavier and heavier
Lie on the floor beside
the thick white ash
Another child gone
The Friday call for prayer
The echo of Imam's voice
You must clean them
You must purify
I have dead sperm

OBEDIENCE

Kneel down in prayer
Allahu Akbar Allahu Akbar
An orgy of pubic hair
Allahu Akbar Allahu Akbar
Bend over torn in half
Allahu Akbar Allahu Akbar
Kneel down in prayer
Allahu Akbar Allahu Akbar
Taste the bittersweet sperm
Allahu Akbar Allahu Akbar
A child is unborn today
Allahu Akbar Allahu Akbar
Kneel down in prayer
Allahu Akbar Allahu Akbar
Forgive me or am I forgiving?
Allahu Akbar Allahu Akbar

AGAINST THE WALL

Grab me / push me against the wall / strap my arms / Lotee / smash my head against the wall / ache / tear / drip / sweat / unzip / trickle / blood / scream / brother / pull them down / Shath / unzip yours / fight another / pop / skin / taste the salty dirt / push / pulsate / pound / gush milky blood / spit / Lotee / walk / forgotten / leave a brother / weep / mother / inhabit a disease / a country's waste / force / forget / throb / hybrid / hide the truth blind people / Lotee search for a truth / lie to hurt another / smile / face / chase the dead / pray on a Friday / chant God / Shath / exert a country's feces / as if it will make me / forget their faces

THE LOTEE WHO FUCKED THE SHATH

The wind shakes my bones to a sheaf

SHAME

SHATH

BANG BANG BANG

HUMAN

The gunshot dissolves in the Lotee

LOTEE

It was the Lotee who fucked the Shath

HALAL

THE MORNINGS I KISSED SADDAM

WHO ARE YOU (I)

You're a
Tight shirt and jeans
Belt out
Angel Gabriel's fly
Erect cock
Amen
Holy shit
Boys dance
God will help you
Fuck in trance bodies
Kneel down and slay
Snort the white
Like Saddam's son Uday

DEPRESSION (I)

He once had a seizure, his hand jolting, tingling goosebumps
When I had a panic attack he took my antidepressants
His existence compulsive key bumps
His voice a weeping cello played in lower range
I met him on his birthday
I knew his friend and yet when I saw him
I saw my whole life through him
I knew he was the one whose tongue interlocks lifelines
His heart numbing skipping a beatless serotonin
His promise the alert and the warning of an apocalyptic war

THE MORNINGS I KISSED SADDAM

There are mornings when I kissed Saddam was at least merciful and forgiving
Hey it's Sunday today The flat thin line of my lips I had a crush on Qusay

LOTEE

There are afternoons when I ate your ass It's 3:11 AM You let me spread your
cheeks wide open You said you support ISIS You fucked me

SHATH

There are nights when you wore the hijab You said I looked beautiful You fed
me shawarma from Abo Ali You smothered me with the flag

BACK TO WHERE WE WERE

There are hair particles on your skin
The kind that made you less Khusrah
If you act like Saddam's son Qusay did when he was drunk
Then you can fuck hypocritically
Don't worry short hairs attract each other
I know I have a foot fetish
I saw the hair on the neighbour's foot
I kept masturbating until I heard her
My mother looked the other way around

SHREDS

Onions shredded piece after piece tear after tear eaten bitter-taste guilty
Lotee but a wedding makes you holy So be ashamed

Look at you aren't you ashamed? Is that what you want to be? A shitty little
Shath? Look at you so dirty so diseased Oh I'm ashamed

I can't even look at your face Let me spit and drool You sick little fucking
Shath Aren't you afraid of Allah?

Eat her pussy Tear her apart Make her wince and cry Push deeper and sigh
I'm sorry I shamed you

Do you want to get the disease and die? Why don't you just die and purify
our family name? You've already brought so much shame

I'm sorry I shamed you I'm sorry I gave you the knife that tore my pink in
half I'm sorry you called me brother I'm sorry I wore the hijab

THE KHUSRAH CONDUCTOR

A Lotee bleeding sperm
Is a Khusrah
The bee sting
Blemished faces
The still waters
Humming mandolin
Anxious insects
The Khusrah sucked the Lotee off
In powder
Shreds of skin
Clouds of hair
The Khusrah thrusts
In the Lotee's floating white
Rain crumbles
On the bloody chatari
Dewdrops drench
Genitals evaporate
The Lotee plucks
The restless fur
Of the bee
And caresses
The Khusrah conductor

WHO ARE YOU? (II)

Your pants
Razor-cut lines of white
Your dick
Fat lines of powder
Your ass
A shot of liquid ecstasy
Your nose
Pepsi-Cola
Your face
White all over
Your feet
Fetish
Obedience

BLOW

Take off your pants and blow
Bang Bang Bang
I can taste your Lotee lips
I can hear my mother's cries
Let me hold your arms Shath
And another says my mother
I can exist in you the other me
Can make them happy
Let me rub against you
But don't taste my sweet vomit
I can feel your rough scruff
But turn your face against this
Let me come to you in joy
The holy prophets of God
I can enjoy the milky-white
Against the heathens
Let me go and forever
Remember God's Jannah

––––––––––

In God's Jannah men shall be attended
By boys graced with eternal youth
The sons of sodomites

Take off your pants and blow
Bang Bang Bang

DEPRESSION (II)

We hid together in a demilitarized zone
The Lotee and Khusrah invisible to others
We stumbled on a hardball smeared ourselves helpless
They stood across from us with their rifles in hand
They yelled foreign threatening the Khusrah understood
They aimed their weapons ready for another kind of war
Kill in the name that will make us both martyrs
My father was a soldier and had fought in the Gulf War
BANG BANG BANG
Together the Lotee held the Khusrah's hand and mourned
We shared a memory of the Shath
I met him on his birthday
We were the same age
He told me to meet him in the bathroom
BANG BANG BANG
I walked inside and he kissed me
We sucked and fucked
I wanted to marry him
BANG BANG BANG

WHO ARE YOU? (III)

Make me dance mister
Let
my
hands immerse   a peacock's feathers in the air
Fifi
Wallah wallah slaughter seven cows
Seven cows   No sir don't chain me
Let me D A N C E
Fifi O beautiful Fifi
I will dance at your marriage   I will
                    Let my hips flow
My marriage
        I'm Fifi   the belly dancer

WHERE IS THE LIGHT?

His Light to whomever He wills
Allah makes metaphors
For mankind
Allah has knowledge
Of all things
But where is my son?
O Allah, where is he?
Where is the knowledge
O God?
From the Pacific to the Tigris

It floats in my arms like Fifi
Before the sacrifice of seven cows
A party in thick blood
Look at Fifi in a white dress
She is married and cheats
What's a man but a man?
He wears a black suit
My people, where is my son?
The olive tree has no light
The kidney through birth
Let Allah make
My son without a wife
A celebration
She would move my fingers
Force my fingers
Inside her pussy
My fingers bleed
On the pearly sand
From the Gulf to Nowhere
From the Gulf

To the holy Karbala

It passes through the blood of Hussain
Fatima, where is my son?
O Hassan, O Ali, O Muhammad
God bless Muhammad and his Family
A clot of snow passes down
Into the Lotee air
Khusrah
Nowhere
Somewhere
This place is me
You are not here
You are not there
But I am here

SHAMEFUL

Are you ashamed?
Pray to Allah
He will heal you
I'm not ashamed

JANNAH

JANNAH (I)

This to tell you that I love you I often thank Allah because He gave me a mother like you Truly you are my guardian angel When you cry my heart bleeds tears When you are happy my heart flies like a caged bird Without you I have a broken wing, crumpled feathers I am he who can't fly but can only weep for his mother I think the most important thing in life is my family and my people More important than anything in the world I know sometimes I say that my career is more important but the truth is it's not Nothing comes close to family I love you all more than anyone else in this world You are my family I remember the night when I stayed with my cousins in Al Halla for a week And you made an unexpected surprise How I missed you and when I saw you Mama my heart skipped a beat I love you

May Allah keep us together now
May Allah protect us from all evils
May Allah make a garden for us
May Allah keep us as one

Afterlife

JANNAH (II)

What about your aunt? Your uncle? You forgot your family, you forgot your people to be dipped in shit in the afterlife. We are family members. We must be together in the afterlife. What is family but a separation? What is the afterlife but a word? Pray to Allah.

I'm scared of the word / Baba
the Afterlife
Jannah

A NOWHERE PLACE

We all want and crave / But it is haram / ask God for love no matter what / laugh like a fag / Are you sure / I'm not ashamed / God Bless / move your hands / What is with you? / What has Shaitan been doing to help? / Today I pulled down my pants I was / anonymous / You're a man / Where do you see another man / fit in

THAT MAN

You threw me in the abyss so let me be anonymous
I am a hyphenated no-one please let me be vulnerable
You let me speak Arabic and English so can I speak in Punjabi
You let me wear the crown of a beauty pageant queen once
You let me dance and imitate Sherihan in her every move
You let me wear the dress you called me a woman
You saw me with a man
You didn't let me be that man

TO MY LOVE

To the man who fucked shit up, an ISIS terrorist, whose white teeth choked me lightly when I let out an explosion of jizz

To my love, the heart that pumped gayness through my veins and spat popsicle into my mouth

To the man who shoved his cock inside my butthole, stretching it, asking if I spoke Arabic

To my love who held my finger and put the ring around it, too tight to fit, and whispered his love for me in Punjabi

To the man who took me in his arms only to turn me around and fuck me from behind

To my love whose arms surrounded me, a gentle kiss on my upper lips, and blew away

To the man who claimed to be ISIS and whose cock was in my mouth when I tasted his semen

To my love who pretended to be straight but fucked me so good behind closed doors

To the man and my love, please know that I'm fed up with living under hypocrisy

To my love I want the world to know of our existence

To the man I cannot hide

SURROGATE

The Sheikh walked with such grace holding the pride flag / He didn't know his name / He would slice off his cock / Feed it to the dogs he said / Why / You're just a Lotee / Do you smell the burning fires / The people of Lut remembered / He liked to choke me sexually as cum spurted out like dragonflies / Thank you to our surrogate mom

Surrogate mom / twins / inshallah / Waheguru / May God protect us from all evils / Lotees & Shaths / Clean the unholy water by cutting their fucking throats off / Baba, I'm the fucking martyr / Do you want to meet your grandchildren? / Thank the surrogate mom/

FAMILY

The umbilical cord
Hangs
The surrogate mother
God is great

The twins hold
Hands
Gay dads
Inshallah & Waheguru

I SEE YOU IN ME

I.

My Prisa
We stand together, looking up at the "Bedouin Princess" and her sapphire
eyes, fragile percussion

2.

My Sipāhī
We hide beneath the gunshot fog and carbon dioxide in an
umbilical cord

3.

My Adhi'āpaka
We pray with our bare hands when Father pulls down his pants in ecstasy

4.

My Citā
We float restlessly unsettling a wave of peacock feathers

5.

My Rāza
We swing weathered hums through the veins of slaughtered
beings

6.

My Basarī
We play music with aching thumbs. Babylonian waters blissfully wash
our sinny sin sins

7.

My Gā'ika
We speak within each other voiceless, mouths raging in intimacy

8.

My Parivāra
We reproduce our skin inside the other particles...

9.

My Prēmī
We tap one beat after another, drum-pounding selfless attachment

10.

My Rūha nū sāthī
We and me and you and I

WAR/TORN

In 1990
I showed you love
In 2011
Love is just a word
In 1990
I fell into your arms
In 2011
Where are your arms?
In 1990
You knew I was different
In 2011
You still know yet deny
In 1990
You had me with you
In 2011
I look for you
In 1990
You needed me and I
In 2011
I really need you but you
In 1990
You could have died but I
In 2011
I would have lived but
In 1990
I was 21 years younger and
In 2011
I was alive and well
In 1990
I was also alive and well

In 2011
I saw myself return
In 1990
I am on my way to you
In 2011
I am alive and well
In 2019
How are you?

Glossary

Adhi'āpaka: teacher

Al Halla: a province in Iraq

Allah yerhamak: "May Allah have mercy on you," usually addressed to the dead

Allahu Akbar: "God is the greatest"

Azan: Islamic call for prayer

Basarī: flute

Chatari: cloth or cover, umbrella made of cloth on iron tiles to avoid rain

Cità: worrier

Eid: a Muslim festivity

El-Sayed: *Sayyid* (also spelled *Syed, Saiyed, Seyit, Seyd, Said, Sayed, Sayyed, Saiyid, Seyed,* and *Seyyed*) (Arabic: سيد [ˈsæj.jɪd], Persian: [sejˈjed]; meaning "Mister"; plural سادة *sādah*) is an honorific title denoting people (*sayyidah* سيده for females) accepted as descendants of the Islamic prophet Muhammad and his cousin Imam Ali through his grandsons, Hasan ibn Ali and Husayn ibn Ali (combined Hasnain), sons of Muhammad's daughter Fatimah and son-in-law Ali (Ali ibn Abi Talib).

Gā'ika: singer

Habibi: my beloved

Hajj: performing the pilgrimage in Mecca, one of the five pillars of Islam

Halal: permitted or lawful in Islam

Haram: forbidden

Jannah: heaven

Inna lillahi wa inna ilayhi raji'un: part of a verse from the Quran that translates to "We belong to God and to Him we shall return." The phrase is commonly recited by Muslims when a person experiences a tragedy, especially upon hearing news that a person has died

Inshallah & Waheguru: "God willing" in Islam and Sikhism

Karar Nushi: Iraqi model and actor killed by radical Islamists for looking gay

Khusrah: a person whose birth sex is male but who identifies as female or as neither male nor female.

Lā'īpha: singer

Lotee: derogatory term for being gay in Arabic. It derives from the story of Lot.

Masjid: mosque

Parivāra: family

Prēmī: premiere
Prisa: prince
Rāza: ray
Rūha nū sāthī: soul companion
Salam: peace
Salat: prayer, one of the five pillars of Islam
Sawm: fasting in Ramadan, one of the five pillars of Islam
Shahadah: the testimony, one of the five pillars of Islam
Shath: queer
Shaitan: Satan
Shayateen: evil spirits
Sipāhī: soldier
Wallah: "I swear to God"
Zakat: charity, one of the five pillars of Islam

Acknowledgements

First and foremost, I want to thank God for the gift called life. I want to thank my parents, Namir and Ghada and my two beautiful sisters Rend and Mays for their unconditional love.

This book began as a chapbook project for English 472 at Simon Fraser University, a course taught by the incredible Jordan Scott, who then continued to help me with the manuscript over the years. Thanks so much Jordan for believing in me from the beginning. Your love and support means the world to me. I'm so thankful to call you my mentor and friend. Thanks so much to Jacqueline Turner for her guidance throughout the workshops in English 372.

I want to thank every single person who has helped me with the edits. I greatly appreciate it. Thanks so much to the extraordinary Shazia Hafiz Ramji for working with me as my editor. You are a genius and you have inspired me so much throughout this journey. Thanks so much as well to Stuart Ross for the excellent copy editing. Also, a huge thank you to Malcolm Sutton for the book cover & layout design.

Thank you so much Jay Millar and Hazel Millar, my incredible publishers at Book*hug Press for believing in my work and for giving me an opportunity I will appreciate forever. It has been so amazing working with you and I look forward to our continued journey together.

To the love of my life, my husband, Tarn, thank you for being the most supportive and for always letting me write. I love you with all my heart.

This book is a voice for the martyrs who have lost their lives because they were different. This book is for every member of the LGBTQ2S community who has faced discrimination for being different. I stand with you all. This book is for you.

HASAN NAMIR was born in Iraq in 1987. He graduated from Simon Fraser University with a BA in English and received the Ying Chen Creative Writing Student Award. He is the author of *God in Pink* (2015), which won the Lambda Literary Award for Best Gay Fiction and was chosen as one of the Top 100 Books of 2015 by *The Globe and Mail*. His work has also been featured on Huffington Post, Shaw TV, Airbnb, and in the film *God in Pink: A Documentary*. He lives with his husband in Vancouver.

Colophon

Manufactured as the first edition of *War/Torn*
in the spring of 2019 by Book*hug Press.

Edited for the press by Shazia Hafiz Ramji
Copy edited by Stuart Ross
Type + design by Malcolm Sutton